CONTENTS

CITIZEN SCIENCE AND BIRDS

Citizen science is a way to help out with scientific research across the world, by taking part in observations and submitting data. Working as citizen scientists, we can observe birds to see how they live and how we can protect their habitats. A large part of researching birds involves identifying species.

ALL BIRDS HAVE ...

Wings
All birds have wings. However, not all birds can fly. Penguins, ostriches and kiwis are all flightless birds.

Beaks
The shape of a bird's beak depends on its diet (see pages 12–13). Birds that eat meat, seeds and fruit will have different shapes of beak.

Feet
The shape of a bird's feet can tell us if it is a land bird or water bird. Water birds have webbed feet to help them push through water. Most birds have four toes, but some have two or three.

Feathers
Birds are the only animals that have feathers. The colour of a bird's feathers can be used as camouflage to hide from predators or sneak up on prey. Male and female birds often have different colour feathers (see page 5).

IDENTIFYING BIRDS

We can use the physical characteristics of birds, such as beak shape, size and colour, to identify them. We can also use other clues such as their habitat and movement. The time of day is important, as some birds are nocturnal. Bird identification books or websites can help us identify birds.

The world's smallest bird is the bee hummingbird, measuring just 5.5 cm.

The world's largest bird is the ostrich with a height of 210 cm.

MALE AND FEMALE

Some male and female birds look different to each other. The most obvious example is the peacock, but there are other common examples, such as ducks. Male birds tend to be more colourful than females. Their bright colours help them to attract a mate.

male duck

female duck

SPECIES SPOTTING

Go on a bird hunt and see how many bird species you can spot in your local area.

Choose a location and a period of time, for example 20 minutes. During this time and in this place, use a bird identification guide to spot different species.

Here are some of the most common birds in towns and cities. You might spot something more unusual if you are in the countryside.

blackbird

Eurasian blue tit

starling

house sparrow

magpie

crow

Keep a tally of the different species you spot and draw a table to present your data. Then, use the Excel program to present your data as a bar chart. Each species is one bar on the graph.

Species	Number of birds seen
Crow	3
Robin	1
Magpie	1
Starling	7

First, copy your data into a spreadsheet in Excel. It should look something like this.

Then, select all of the cells that contain data and click the 'Charts' button. Choose the 'Bar' option. This will create a bar chart from your data.

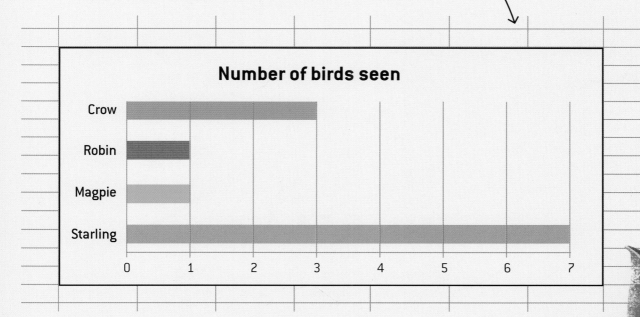

Number of birds seen

Crow — 3
Robin — 1
Magpie — 1
Starling — 7

(x-axis: 0 1 2 3 4 5 6 7)

GET INVOLVED!

You can upload your research to an official bird count, such as The Great Backyard Bird Count (gbbc.birdcount.org/help-faqs/#where) or the Big Garden Bird Watch (www.rspb.org.uk/get-involved/activities/birdwatch/). Check in advance as they may ask for the count to take place on a certain date.

BIRD HABITATS

Birds can be found in almost every habitat around the world. They live on land and on water, and in hot and cold conditions.

ADAPTATIONS

Birds have adapted to be better suited to the conditions in their habitats. These adaptations help them to survive. For example, birds that live in cold habitats have layers of fat and feathers that trap air for insulation. Birds are often able to tuck one leg up while resting to keep themselves as warm as possible.

LIVING TOGETHER

Birds of the same species often live together in colonies in the same habitat. There is safety in numbers, as the risk of an attack from a predator for each individual is reduced. Birds can also stand together for warmth and help groom each other.

HABITATS AT RISK

Many bird habitats are threatened by human activity. The areas where they live are being destroyed for farmland or to build homes and businesses. Birds depend on trees for food and shelter, so cutting down trees has a huge impact on them.

POLLUTION

Pollution is also a great threat to birds, especially when it contaminates their habitat. They get sick when they consume pesticides and chemicals that are dumped on land or in water. Birds are often confused by rubbish and plastic waste. They think that it is food and eat it, which damages their insides and can kill them.

CONFUSION AND STRESS

Noise and light pollution have a serious impact on birds and their habitats. Noise from factories and airports can confuse birds and make them stressed. This means that birds leave noisy areas, which reduces biodiversity (the number of different species in an area). Light at night from homes and businesses confuses nocturnal birds, such as owls. They don't know when to go out and hunt and can go hungry.

MAKE A FACT FILE

Get out into your local area and research which birds live in different habitats. Spot how different species adapt to their habitat.

Choose three habitats in your local area, such as a city centre, a park, a beach, a woodland area or a lake. Try to make them as different as possible.

park

pond or lake

city centre

Spend 30 minutes exploring each habitat with an adult. Observe the birds that live there and fill in a fact file with the data that you collect. If you have any gaps, use a bird identification guide to help you (shown in brackets in the fact files).

GET INVOLVED!

While you are in each habitat, see if it is affected by human activity. Can you see any rubbish, noise or light that might be affecting the bird population? If so, get involved to solve the problem! Why not organise a litter-picking hour to clean up the rubbish or send an email to your MP or local wildlife charity about your concerns?

FACT FILES

Location	Bird species	Shelter/Nest location	Diet	Movement
City centre	Pigeon			
City centre	Seagull			
City centre	Crow			

Location	Bird species	Shelter/Nest location	Diet	Movement
Beach	Seagull			
Beach	Wood sandpiper			
Beach	Gannet			

Location	Bird species	Shelter/Nest location	Diet	Movement
Park	Pigeon	Trees	Rubbish, seeds, fruit	Flying, walking
Park	Seagull	(Cliffs)	Rubbish, (fish and small animals)	Flying, walking, (swimming)
Park	Magpie	Trees	Insects fruit	Flying, walking

When you've completed your fact files for each habitat, turn your results into a Venn diagram. This diagram will show which birds only live in one type of habitat and which birds live in two or more.

- Draw three large overlapping circles and label each one with the name of a habitat.

- If a bird only appears in one habitat, write its name inside the circle that represents that habitat.

- If a bird appears in two habitats, write its name in the space between the two circles that represent those habitats.

- If a bird appears in all three habitats, write its name in the centre of all three circles.

- Colouring the different sections helps to make the Venn diagram easier to read.

park

city centre

magpie

pigeon

seagull

wood sandpiper

crow

gannet

beach

BIRD DIETS

Different species of birds have different diets. Some eat other animals, such as small mammals or insects, while others eat fruit, seeds and even plant nectar.

Birds of prey have sharp, hooked beaks to tear meat.

Ducks have comb-like beaks to strain insects and plants out of the water.

BEAK SHAPE

The shape of a bird's beak is a good clue as to the kind of food they eat. Over millions of years, their beaks have adapted (changed) so that they have the perfect shape for the food available in their area.

Swallows have short, tweezer-like beaks to snatch insects out of the air.

Cardinals have short, cone-shaped beaks to crack open nuts and seeds.

Hummingbirds have long, needle-like beaks to reach into flowers for nectar.

Birds can be found at different stages of food webs. They eat species that are lower down the food web, such as plants, small insects and animals. They also provide food for other animals, including birds of prey and large mammals.

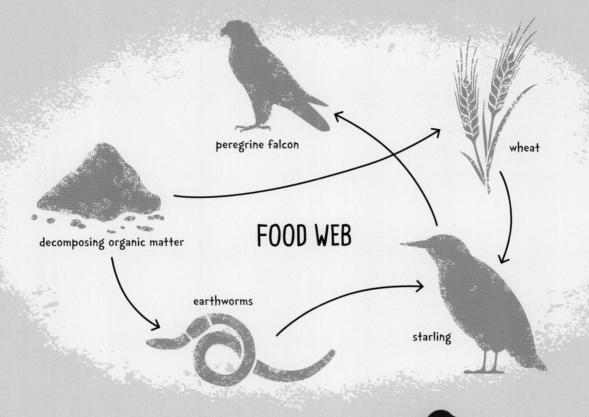

peregrine falcon

wheat

decomposing organic matter

FOOD WEB

earthworms

starling

GOING HUNGRY

Bird diets are affected by climate change and human activity. When fruit grows earlier in the season because of warm weather, it can leave birds hungry later in the year. When farm pesticides kill insects, there is less food for insect-eating birds.

TEST BEAK ADAPTATIONS

Try this experiment to see different beak adaptations in action. Use household tools to test how different shapes of beak are best at collecting different types of food.

YOU WILL NEED:

A bowl of rice (to represent small seeds)

A bowl of pistachios (to represent large seeds in shells — these need to be broken open)

A bowl of 5-cm-long pieces of string buried in soil (to represent worms)

A string with marshmallows threaded on to it (to represent fruit)

Tweezers

Chopsticks

Pliers

Scissors

Paper cups

/// WARNING ///
BE CAREFUL HANDLING SCISSORS

You have 30 seconds to gather as much food as possible using each tool (or beak) and transfer it to a paper cup. The cup represents the bird's stomach. Draw a chart to keep track of how much you can collect using each tool.

	Tweezers	Chopsticks	Pliers	Scissors
Rice	6	2	0	0
Pistachios	2	1	4	1
String	2	4	1	2
Marshmallows	2	1	3	4

Once you have finished, present your data in a pie chart. Draw one pie chart for each type of food to show which tool is best at picking it up.

Pistachios	
Tool	Number collected
Tweezers	2
Chopsticks	1
Pliers	4
Scissors	1

First, copy your data into a spreadsheet in Excel. It should look something like this.

Then, select all of the cells that contain data and click the 'Charts' button. Choose the 'Pie' option. This will create a pie chart from your data.

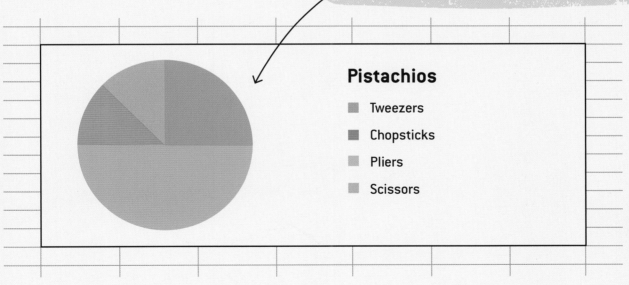

Pistachios

■ Tweezers
■ Chopsticks
■ Pliers
■ Scissors

TRY IT! Can you think of other bird beaks that can be represented by tools? You could use a slotted spoon to represent a duck's beak or a straw to represent a hummingbird's beak. Repeat this experiment with the new beaks and foods commonly eaten by those birds, such as gummy sweets in a bowl of water to represent fish or frogs, or water to represent nectar.

BUILDING A NEST

Birds are born from eggs of many colours and sizes. Many female birds lay eggs in nests. They often lay more than one egg at once.

MATERIALS

Different birds build their nests from different materials, including grass, leaves, mud, branches and moss. They use materials that are available in the habitat where they live. Some birds build their nests in specially adapted shapes to keep their eggs safe from predators or to suit the conditions in which they live.

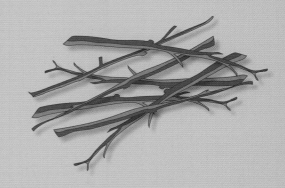

Pigeons build their nests in trees or on rooftops.

White storks build nests on chimneys or electrical poles.

Weaver bird nests have an opening at the bottom so predators can't find their way in.

INSIDE AN EGG

The eggs that we eat are unfertilised. They only contain egg white and an egg yolk. If an egg is fertilised by a male bird, a chick grows inside the egg. The egg white and egg yolk provide nutrients for the chick. Eggs have a hard shell to protect the soft insides.

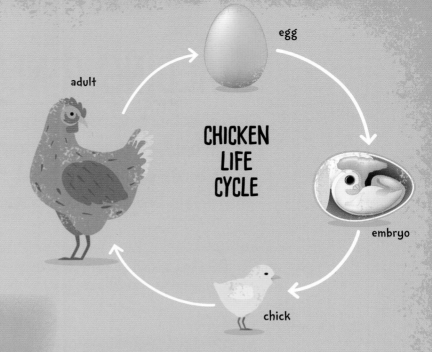

CHICKEN LIFE CYCLE

egg

adult

embryo

chick

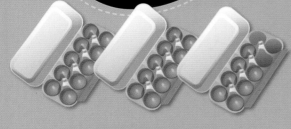

1.4 kg
the weight of one ostrich egg

**that's the same as
27 CHICKEN EGGS!**

BREAKING OUT

Bird eggs need to be incubated (kept warm) while chicks are growing inside. Birds often do this by sitting on or near their eggs in the nest. When the chicks are ready to hatch, they break through the egg shell using a bump on their beak called an egg tooth.

GROWING UP

Some chicks can look after themselves as soon as they hatch. Others have to stay in the nest for a while, and their parents bring them food. Once they have learned how to fly or fend for themselves, they leave the nest and live on their own.

HOW BIRDS FLY

Birds flap their wings to fly. Flying looks effortless but it requires a complicated balance of forces.

IN A FLAP

Birds use muscles in their chest to flap their wings up and down. This creates the force of thrust, which pushes the bird forwards and upwards. The bird's thrust needs to be greater than the air resistance, which is the force pulling back on the bird as it flies.

DOWN-STROKE

The down-stroke provides the majority of the thrust.

UP-STROKE

At each up-stroke the wing is slightly folded in to reduce air resistance and save energy.

WING SHAPE

Wings are curved at the top and flat along the bottom. This means that air travels a longer distance as it passes over the top of the wing. This reduces air pressure above the wing and increases air pressure below the wing. The greater air pressure below the wing creates lift, which pushes the bird upwards.

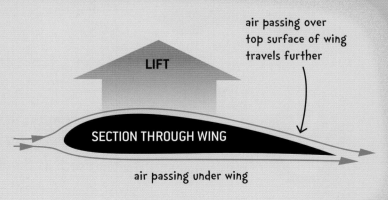

air passing over top surface of wing travels further

LIFT

SECTION THROUGH WING

air passing under wing

FEATHERS

Long, stiff feathers on the wings, known as flight feathers, have a streamlined shape. This allows the bird's wings to flap through the air with less resistance. Birds use the feathers in their tail to steer from side to side.

LIGHT AS AIR

Birds need to be as light as possible so that they don't have to work as hard to stay floating in the air. They have hollow bones to reduce their weight. Their bones are filled with air and tiny bars of bone to stop the bone from collapsing inwards.

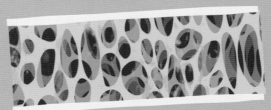

close-up section of a bird's bone

DIFFERENT STYLES

Some birds fly in different ways.

During migration (see pages 24–25), some birds, such as the albatross, save energy by using currents of warm air to keep them moving without flapping their wings. This is called gliding.

Hummingbirds flap their wings more than 40 times a second, which allows them to hover in place while collecting nectar.

Some birds, such as puffins, even flap their wings underwater to dive while hunting.

OBSERVE AN OIL SPILL

Oil can be spilled into the ocean from ships and oil drilling platforms. The oil in the water has a very serious impact on ocean animals, including birds. Recreate an oil spill in a container and see how it affects feathers.

YOU WILL NEED:

Two deep trays

Water

A real feather from a craft shop

Vegetable oil

Washing up liquid

///// WARNING /////

FEATHERS THAT YOU FIND OUTDOORS CAN CARRY DISEASES, SO IT'S BEST TO USE FEATHERS FROM A CRAFT SHOP FOR THIS PROJECT.

Fill one of the trays with water. Place one of the feathers in the water and observe what happens. Does the feather float or sink? Take the feather out of the water and observe it. Is the feather damp or dry? Write down your observations.

Pour some vegetable oil into the tray of water. Place the feather back into the tray and observe what happens. Does it behave in the same way as it did in the tray with just water?

Fill the second tray with water. Remove the feather from the tray of oil and water and place it in the water. Again, record how the feather behaves.

TRY IT!

Try to clean the feather with water. Is that enough to remove the oil? What happens if you use a small amount of washing up liquid?

Write up your observations. Can you think of a reason why feathers behave in this way? Read on to find out why!

WHY?

- Feathers are waterproof. They repel water to keep birds warm. They will float on the surface of water because they are so light.

- When oil enters the ocean, it does not mix with the water. Instead, it floats on top. When birds float on the surface of the water, they get covered in oil.

- As you will have observed, when feathers are covered in oil, they don't float or repel water. This makes it hard for birds to float, keep warm and fly.

- Birds will try to clean the oil off their feathers, but it is very hard, as water and spit aren't enough to remove it. They end up eating a lot of oil, which makes them ill. The only way to clean off the oil is with detergents, such as washing up liquid. Specialist teams clean up animals after an oil spill, but there are many that they can't save.

MIGRATION

Migration is a long journey that some birds make every year. They often live in one place in the winter and another place in the summer.

SURVIVAL

Birds migrate to survive. They migrate to avoid cold weather, to find new sources of food and safe places to breed. They return to the same places every year.

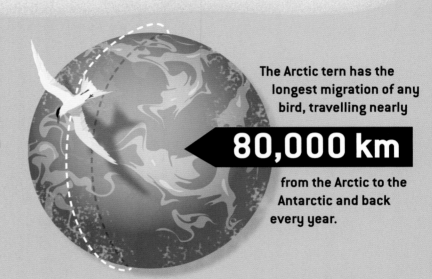

The Arctic tern has the longest migration of any bird, travelling nearly

80,000 km

from the Arctic to the Antarctic and back every year.

ROUTES

Birds follow the same migration routes every year, crossing countries, oceans and even continents. Some species fly non-stop, while others stop to rest.

FLOCKS AND FORMATION

During migration, birds often travel in groups called flocks. There is safety in numbers from predators. They sometimes fly together in a V-shape. The bird flying at the front breaks up the wall of air, so that there's less air resistance for the birds flying behind.

A flock of twenty-five birds flying in a V formation can fly **70% FURTHER** than a bird flying alone.

CHANGING SEASONS

Climate change is affecting migration. Unseasonably warm weather confuses birds and can make them migrate at an earlier date. When they arrive, it may be too early for food to be available, and so they go hungry.

PROJECT

FOLLOW BIRD MIGRATION

Record bird populations over a year and see migration in action.

Research and choose a migratory bird species that definitely visits the place where you live. Here are some common migratory species that might come to your local area.

swallow
(Northern Hemisphere to Southern Hemisphere)

Atlantic puffin
(Atlantic ocean to northern Atlantic coastlines)

arctic tern
(Arctic to Antarctic)

western sandpiper
(Alaska to USA coastlines)

Canada goose
(northern North America to southern North America and Europe)

Once a week, at the same time and in the same place, spend 10 minutes looking out for the species that you chose. Choose a place where you have seen these birds previously or a location where there are lots of birds, such as a park or nature reserve. Count how many of the migrating species you spot and write down the number.

Repeat this activity every week for a whole year! If you can't manage to go bird spotting every week, why not try going every two weeks? Remember that these birds are migratory, so there will be periods in which you don't see them. You could use this time to spot other birds but you can't include these results in your data.

Once you have collected your data, present it in a line graph. The line goes up and down to show how the population changes over the year.

First, copy your data into a spreadsheet in Excel. It should look something like this.

Then, select all of the cells that contain data and click the 'Charts' button. Choose the 'Line' option. This will create a line graph from your data.

Swallows	
Week	Number
1	0
2	0
3	0
4	0
5	0
6	0
7	0
8	0
9	0
10	0
11	0
12	0
13	0
14	0
15	3
16	5
17	5
18	12
19	9
20	15

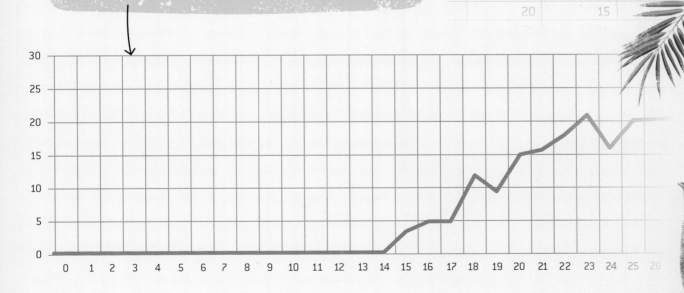

GET INVOLVED!

You can add your data to bigger migration research projects, such as https://ebird.org/home. Why not repeat your research next year and compare the dates? Do the birds arrive and leave at roughly the same time?

KEEP IT FAIR

All of the projects in this book will help you to learn more about birds in your local area and how to protect them. However, it's important for you to make your experiments fair. If you don't control the different elements of an experiment, the results won't be accurate and won't mean anything.

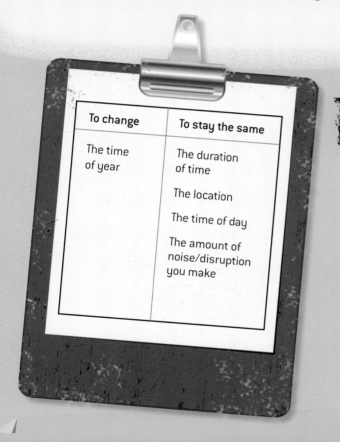

To change	To stay the same
The time of year	The duration of time
	The location
	The time of day
	The amount of noise/disruption you make

VARIABLES

There are lots of elements in experiments. These are called the variables. To make an experiment a fair test, you can only change one variable. All other variables have to stay the same. For example, in the migration project on pages 26–27, the only variable you are changing is the time of year. Everything else should stay the same.

INACCURATE RESULTS

If you have more than one variable, you won't know which one has affected your results. For example, if you counted birds at night in February, you wouldn't know if the low number of birds was because of the month or because of the time of day. This makes your research invalid.

PLAN AHEAD

It's important to plan how you will make your experiment fair before you begin. This helps to keep the variables the same throughout. Write down important details, such as lengths of time, so that you don't forget.

OVER TO YOU!

When you've finished the projects in this book, why not make up your own?

First, you need to think of an idea that you want to test. This is called the hypothesis. For example:

'I THINK THAT SMALL BIRDS PREFER TO EAT SMALL SEEDS.'

Next, think about your variables — what will you keep the same and what will you change?

Then, carry out your experiment. You should repeat it a few times to make sure that your results aren't a one-off. Present your ideas using one of the graphs from the book. Finally, use your results to come up with a conclusion — what do the results show you? Was your hypothesis right or wrong?

GLOSSARY

adaptation a way in which a living thing has changed over many years to be better suited to its environment

air pressure the force of air pressing on an area

air resistance a force that slows objects down as they move through the air

biodiversity the number of different species in an area

camouflage having a colour or pattern that is similar to the surroundings so it is difficult to see

colony a group of the same type of animals that live together

conclusion the opinion you have after finding out all of the information necessary

fertilised a fertilised egg has cells from the male and female bird and will develop into a chick

glide to fly by floating on air currents instead of by flapping wings

groom to clean an animal

hypothesis an idea that needs to be tested

incubate to keep eggs warm

insulation something that stops heat from escaping

mate an animal's partner with which they will have young

migrate to travel to a different place when the season changes

nocturnal an animal that is active at night and rests during the day

pesticide a chemical used to kill unwanted animals or plants

predator an animal that kills and eats other animals

prey an animal that is hunted and killed by other animals

repel to make something move away

streamlined something with a smooth shape that can easily move through air or water

tally a running total

thrust a force that pushes something forwards

variable an element in an experiment that can change

FURTHER INFORMATION

BOOKS

Birds *Classifying Animals*
By Sarah Wilkes,
Wayland, 2014

Birds *The Great Nature Hunt*
By Cath Senker
Franklin Watts, 2016

Illustrated Compendium of Birds
By Virginie Aladjidi and
Emmanuelle Tchoukriel,
Franklin Watts, 2016

WEBSITES

www.rspb.org.uk/birds-and-wildlife/wildlife-guides/identify-a-bird
Identify UK birds using the RSPB bird identifier.

www.audubon.org/get-outside/activities
Discover DIY projects and activities to help birds.

www.bbc.com/bitesize/clips/zx4rkqt
Watch a video about birds of prey.

INDEX